CW00531069

THE VIEW FROM
THE STOCKADE

THE VIEW FROM
THE STOCKADE

Landeg White

Dangaroo Press

Acknowledgments are due to the editors of *Poetry Review*, *Poetry Wales*, *Southern African Review of Books*, *Stand* and to the *1985 Anthology of the Avon Poetry Competition* where some of these poems first appeared.

The lines quoted on p. 31 are from Sir Richard Fanshawe's translation of Luis Vaz de Camões, *The Lusiads*, ed. Geoffrey Bullough (Centaur Press Ltd, 1963)

© Landeg White, 1991

First published in 1991 by Dangaroo Press,
Australia: G.P.O. Box 1209, Sydney NSW 2001
Denmark: Pinds Hus, Geding Søvej 21, 8381 Mundelstrup.
UK: P.O. Box 186 Coventry CV4 7HG

Typeset by Robert Vicat Ltd,
25a Greencroft Gardens, London NW6 3LN

ISBN 1 871049 22 9

For MARIA ALICE
as before
and for
JACK

CONTENTS

Alcabideche
(etc)

HERE
(Maputo etc)

Incident at a Poetry Reading

(for Eduardo White, *primo*)

In the old walled garden the young poets
Have spread laden tables under the mango tree.
We stand reverently in the starving city

Eyeing the roast suckling pig, samousas,
Fried prawns, chicken with groundnut sauce,
Goat piri-piri, wines and beers,

While the speech from the dais about the young
Poets' aspirations reaches its peroration
In a *caldeirada* of revolutionary slogans,

And we clap, our hands straining to do
What they do next, reaching out for food
And drink until all the tables are cleared

And we stretch our legs under the mango tree,
A black silence in the glistening sky,
Enjoying the young poets' newest poetry.

Eduardo is long-limbed. He bears signs
Of his mother's tenderness. His sudden
Manhood has tightened like a skin.

His poem is angry. The nation is a neglected
Garden rank with rotting fruits. Corruption
And our silence are forfeiting victories.

We watch him touched on the shoulder
By uniformed men. He falters in his reading.
Detention without trial has its own prosody.

But "Talk!" they insist. "You are telling truths,"
And the poem ends wildly with kisses and applause
And the evening in an afterglow of pleasure,

Beer bottles clinking in the mango tree's shadow,
Talk about language and the international standard,
Tiny green mangoes dropping on our bare heads,

While beyond the *bairros* past the airport road
Despairing peasants flock to the city for food
And the siege tightens with mutilation and murder.

Living in the Delta

    Darkness,
A wet tarpaulin weighing
Down the mangrove, moulders
To a yellow fog, threadbare at dawn.
The fishermen stir from the fire,
Their cigarettes trailing candleflies,
Then slither narrow dugouts under
Roots pale with oysters into the warm
Crocodile waters of the creek.
After all these years of words it is still
Discovery, the canopy whitening
Over the surf, the silver glimmering beach
And a medieval sea where pelicans
Loom on a sandbank and these fishermen
Like the centuries rock patiently
At anchor.
    Noon,
The sand vines blazing
Purple and the white-hot sand
Whistling to my heels, I found
Her in the hollow where a coconut bole
Strained at its roots, the palm's shadow
Dark at the wreck's charred ribs
On the headland, clasping becalmed
The length of her olive body. She
To whom all metaphors return lay
Strange and familiar, the gold
And tawny chevrons shifting only
To her breathing. Swamp, strand, the bayscape
Taut as a drum.
    Dusk
And a walk around the liberated
Playground, the swing seats
Unchained, the see-saw bending,
The toadstool tables turned. Feverish
In twilight the estate house
Crumbles. The Piper revs for take-off,

Cantering down the golf course, barking
Scottie in pursuit. We along the flood
Defences saunter to the club. Fires
Glisten from the compounds where
Shoeless children sing of blood,
Their guns of bamboo slung across
Bare navels.
    Night,
The swamp road to Hotel *Chuabo*:
Suits, fountains, canned music,
Dinner like an airport cafe, varnish
Flaking from the wardrobe door. But
Chuabo, meaning stockade, the town's
Peasant name, has an eighth-storey
Balcony for drinking. Far above
The masses, over the blacked-out *bairros*,
Russian experts, acrobats from Pyongyang
And we, separately expatriate, shuttered
With glass and the drifting stars,
Meditate on the salt-logged coconut,
Swamps of water hyacinth, the mouldering
Steps at dusk where hippos boom
From the papyrus and the river lurks, waiting
Its season, silted in the lifetimes
Of some of us … Each of us
Rises in this stockade, far from ambush
And famine, to meet the kindly liberators.
They are correctly bearded and smiling.

Scribble

So, the Swedes the blonde gods have abdicated,
the push-button saw-mill is abandoned.

In its twilight, mildew summons
vox humana of mosquitoes.

Outside in the day glare the far bank
fades to sepia, its fringe of palms dancing.

They were planning ho! ho! ho! these tall efficient
vikings with their bearded earnestness

that anthill and baobab, the river drifting with its
                                islands, the flapping herds
trumpeting down the mushroom huts and hut-high millet

be sawn, sanded, cooled, refined
to a white rectangle of paper like this one.

They are not the first
whose blank eden sprung a serpent.

Sugar men, copra men, tea, sizal, tobacco men
have all before loaded their ships and departed.

There are ruined engines of antiquarian value
corroding on all the river estates,

but nothing so fine as the saw-mill
shining blonde at the farm's edge, where a woman

hunchbacked with child is hoeing poverty,
still waiting for a god prepared to scribble.

From Robert Moffat's Journal, 1854

"4th June, Sabbath: the afternoon
cloudy and cold. Under the *mosetla* tree
I once addressed Senthuhe and his men.
The whole town has been burned off
by the Boers. No piles of stones,
broken pillars, tesselated pavements,
nor the shadow of a street, nor anything,
remain to tell 1000s once lived here.
Charred stumps peep here and there
through the ground, with two or three
skulls shot cruelly by the Boers,
and cats too, said one, watching my kittens.

Sebobi, hearing of waggons, came down
from the summit and his people emerged.
After coffee, I assembled them and preached.
I talked with him on the importance
of attending to divine things but, alas,
he is very far from the kingdom of God.

All will be ordered by Him who knows
our hairs' number and sees the sparrows fall
(there are no sparrows here. I had thought
them everywhere. Like flies and crows)."

Cotton, Rubber, Tobacco etc

"So now you are going to have your coffee?"
Says the interpreter approvingly,
And the villagers gather in a noisy circle to study
The white man drinking his coffee.

They have all grown coffee for the white man
And can tell me about every stage
Of the culture and preparation — except for the drinking
Which is hilarious to watch.

Who knows? Next I might change my underpants,
Blow up a condom, burn
A cigar, or do something else they have worked
Lives for and never earn.

Swamp

The Lodge is adventitious, cantilevered
between rocks, a place for adultery.
Even before the black lake rose
to claim it, couples wondered
at dusk as the fever trees grew luminous.

On offer were the tropics, swollen
fruit, ravaged blossoms, the sun
wrecked among coconuts. It took
topsoil and sprinklers to import
such metaphors. And then the lake rose.

Today you can wade past the sand-
bagged chalets to the barbed fence
where Africa resumes. Girls bathe
in the swamp among the blue waterlilies,
squealing satirically as they catch you watching.

Chimwalira

The truth is he was born at Chimwalira
Not Bethlehem. For Immanuel the conception
Was a good one. But it was hard in a place
Without writing to show prophecies fulfilled.
She gave birth on a reed mat in a mud house,
But so did every woman. How much grander
A stable signifying property in the foreground.
So when the Magi appalled by the Nile's
Green wilderness turned back worshipping
A Jewish boy in a safe colony, they missed
Their star's conjunction with Crux Australis
And God lay forgotten in Africa.
                              Chimwalira,
"Where someone died". He grew up ordinarily,
Neither Tarzan nor Shaka, eating millet
And wild mice. After his circumcision
There were songs about his dullness with women.
He became a blacksmith and a doctor skilled
In exorcism, and people saw he was touched.
But there was nothing startling to the elders
In his proverbs. He died old at thirty-three,
A normal life span.
            (It was the Reverend Duff McDuff
Screamed the Python Priest was the Black Christ
As they led him to his steamer in their straightjacket.)

Words for Heroes' Day, perhaps

Being in the Welsh style uninclined to give politicians
Credit for the brilliant acts their speeches enjoin us
To applaud on their tightrope strung between banks,

Nor finding congenial the climate of cenotaphs,
Rituals of death as though death were sacrifice
And sacrifice legitimised those hierachies of stamping,

Not being, in short, in any sense *imbongi* or praise poet,
Whether sweeping thorns from the ruler's path or brandishing
A symbolic knobkerrie as spokesman for the people,

I am in the English manner a little at a loss to find
Words for this anniversary when visiting after Empire
I am asked to pay tribute to those who died for Freedom.

That some were heroes is quite certain though not
Necessarily the men on the platform (nor necessarily men).
Even the dead are ambiguous. Remembering them I think

Most of those innocents cremated in their hundreds
As fire rained on the camps where they were queuing for flour.
Calling them heroes makes their slaughter seem called for

Though their ghosts cry out for an eternal flame of anger.
Even among the warriors there were, as we too well understood,
The psychopathic who will never settle to justice.

But though irony has no heroes there is a poetry of facts.
There were others (not necessarily the men on the platform)
Who are already legend and their legend a gracious one,

Speaking of pastoral, the column filing through the tall
Grass to a clearing with huts in the hut-high millet
And a shining welcome from the old who remembered the Rising,

Speeches, courtesies observed with prayers to the ancestors,
Songs and dancing, the girls crazy with admiration,
The meal from a shared pot when even a bean was divided,

Then at moonrise moving onwards to the dawn's target,
And though doubting whether half of this happened or whether
Half of that half matters in the unchanged city,

I honour them for the metaphors they died for. That
They made strutting ridiculous, if only momentarily,
Is sufficient for our homage. May their ghosts

Snatch at these anklets rattling today for our applause.

Waiting for the Funeral

Those honourably buried with the dead King
Alive (before this glorious present) were
Concubines, fowl-catchers, panderers, slaves.
How could he travel into darkness unsolaced
By those who had greased his lifetime? An hour
After the burial, the earth still shifted.

They scrape and curtsey this President's
Hangers-on as he boasts of the glorious past.
And us? We're waiting for the funeral.

The Accord

The ambassador's wife greets with a kiss
Xavier, pot-bellied, hair growing out of his ears.

In his slim heyday he founded a dozen newspapers
And lost interest in them. The secret police

Of six dictatorships had him on their files
Though his insignificance kept him out of their jails.

Now he's a ranconteur with a whisky in his hand,
A man to be courted, the right ear of the President.

He has been comrade to an alphabet of revolutionaries:
Amilcar, a true marxist despite the controversies,

David who turned to the bottle when his poetry dried up,
Eduardo, Herbert, Marcelino, Philipe,

And Samora the victor whom, after fourteen years
Of excoriating defectors, he advised to make peace

(Though Nelson and Walter were still on Robben Island).
Xavier is writing a book about necessity and the dialectic

And his own career in cellars and public libraries,
Those endless trains, third class, across central Europe,

And an article explaining about Dar es Salaam
Based on Lazaro's letters and a diary kept at the time,

And a pamphlet analysing why the nation is in crisis.
The ambassador's wife is glassy-eyed listening to this.

The whisky-bottle's hourglass has too long to run.
"How can you know," she says, "the right people will win?"

Xavier is disconcerted. He is not used to disagreement.
He was hardly aware there was a woman present.

"How do you stop it ending in a lot of nastiness?"
Is she a liberal? Or just stupid? A waste

Of time explaining. He searches for Latin courtesy
Just as she too is remembering necessity

And they smile like conspirators as she reaches
For the bottle, pours two fingers and signals the kitchen.

Theoretician-pragmatist, Xavier bows to the accord,
Gets a peck at departure as his gallantry award.

Incident from an Archive

Confidentially in Zomba in December '36,
Flatteringly assured of their man-to-man goodwill
(This being a council of the leaders of men),
The D.C. told the District Chiefs
King Edward had abdicated "through illness".

Illness? *Koma e*? Didn't they have men
In the mines, in *ku-Joni*, where there were
Newspapers, radios, boss boys mocking?
The chiefs were solicitous. Poor Bwana,
Worried his harangues about blood and discipline

Would look damn silly if the truth were told.
None of them would abdicate for a woman, even
An American. So they closed ranks, hoping
The Empire would holding, hoping
King Edward would be "cured by Madam Simpisoni".

Thief

The heat is on. We sleep
naked, starting at broken glass.

What will he feel the slippery
Thief interrupted in the living room

Who has kept me hours by the smashed
Door with his sharpened cutlass,

What will be his rage he grabbed
Only the Bassoon Concerto K191?

Benighted under a toenail moon
The tin roof sighs, contracting.

The fridge offs. In shocking quiet
A cockroach smacks the lampshade.

The nightjar whistles like someone
Jumping sing-sing on a wire fence.

I am tuned for violence. I make
Arpeggios with the cutlass. Images are

That head and hand through the jagged
Frame and my striking bloodily.

Nightlong I appease witches.
With cockcrow the denials cease.

But what of him in his mud shack
In the *bairro* angry with Mozart?

Beauty, patronage, such order: shivering
He might well come back to kill.

24

Episode in a War:
Mozambique 1972

"Give me a poem equal to the deeds
Of your brave Servitors."
(Camões: *Os Lusiadas*)

1

It was a baby, weeks old and white,
Cocooned in cotton, nursing its
Pink thumb in the mealie basket
Under the mosquito curtain. As she slung
Across her shoulder the AK 47
Yelling to the comrades to stop smashing
Furniture, she pressed the child
To her battlegreen tunic, laughing.

Greylight. An orchard of oranges
Sloped to the river. Mist
Whitened the globes. Mist
Like the silversmith's hammered escudo
Hung filigree on barbed wire. Over
Exploding heads of papyrus it menaced
Horizontal. A gun butt stove
In the houseboy's resistance.

"*Onde forão?* Where they go?"
"Bwana." He coughed blood. Clasping
The baby she made herself watch.
"Bwana." Another thud. "I'm not
Your bwana, comrade!" Laughter
At Comrade China's joke. "This man
A big stooge, isn't it?" She pushed
Between them. "Tell me the baby's name."

The old man looked astonished.

His eyes betrayed him, flicking
To the papyrus then willed
Back to the carpet, sweat
Gleaming on his bald head. Carefully
He spat blood into a white
Handkerchief. "Moises Ernesto," he
Muttered. "You must give me the boy."

Under the white mist the river slid
Motionless. The guerrillas stared
Blankly. The launch had gone,
The overseer escaped. Mosquitoes
Drifted, neutered by the cold.
Back at the house where sunrise
Flamed in the windows the old man
Repeated, "You must give the boy to me."

2

Swamp and corrugation. She was not meant
To be outside. Five days they kept her
Drugged in the customs house in the delta.
She lay on a white sheet in a cotton shift.
Five noons shimmered the island to sepia
Squinnying her pupils though her blue eyes stared.
She was grounded metres above the brown river.
At dusk, husbanded impatiently, she watched
Evening wrecked on a reef of coconut palms.
Day six, Ernesto shrank from his pale wife
Getting drunk in a village near Mathilde
Where satirical women opened their blouses
To give suck to the white man. That evening
She walked in her white shift to the beach.
Rust and detritus, the channel gouged
Between hulks, the jetty a swamped freighter,
Foredeck clutched by hands of mangrove, hold
Bottomless with writhing embryos it had
Dizzied her to stare down as she disembarked
While, sunk around her on the beach, sand

26

Combed through her languid fingers was rust
Of bolts, rivets, pipes, boilers, anchors,
Buoys, steel plates, hinges, flaking, crumbling
Like driftwood, dissolving. Clouds blazed
Above the coconut flags. A dugout fought
The current with ringing solo and undertow
From six chanting paddlers. Flashes of pink
Were flamingoes returning. The first mosquito
She stamped her name ISOBEL on the white sand
In the hightide slick where banana roots,
Oil seeds, clumps of water hyacinth reeked
Of reeds upriver where he forgot her baby.

3

Cold moonbeams filled the cave
Like a searchlight. The comrades
Slumped, angry with the baby
And her ceaseless lullaby. Down
The track where they had flung
Skulls and the cooking pots,
They could still hear hyena
Houseboy coughing behind a boulder.

In the cave's ash was their
Bomb. It had nose-coned safely
In a green rice paddy and they had
Dragged it here on a mat of baobab
Bark. The cave of burials
Was their hiding place, tossing
Downhill old bones to prove
The revolution stronger than witches.

"*Camarada*, this is not correct,
You must analyse the situation."
For a hunted week she would
Not part with Moises Ernesto
And stooge had tracked down
All their secrets. "Kill him,"

She answered. She was outvoted.
Hyena was salvation for the baby.

In the moonblanched valley the river
Brimmed with islands spinning
South to the delta. The baby
Slept. Each quick
Breath she held hers awaiting
His next. Her eyes avoided
The cave's blank vault where
Guns impaled her shadow. "We are all

Bewitched," said Comrade China.
She answered again, "I will
Give Moises Ernesto to his mother."
"How? By helicopter? You will
Drop him by parachuter?" The cave
Darkened. The old man
Stood in the entrance holding
Skulls. "I have a plan," he said.

4

Ernesto woke with a headache on the mud floor.
He was going to beat that woman. He knew
What the terrorists did to Moises Ernesto.
They tossed him on their bayonets. They played
Volleyball on the lawn with his little head.
He was a man. He had to exist knowing
Such things. But she? A man needed comfort
When his baptised son was murdered, not
This deafening with silence. Go back
Upriver? Fighting the current with the green
Ambush waiting and the boy already dead?
His Excellency the Governor said, "Ernesto,
Condolences, you did well to save the launch."
He was going to punish that woman. Not
Tell her, that would be cruel. Only men
Lived with knowledge. But teach her duty

Like this woman with water from the river
And a rag to wash his prick and firewood
To roast his breakfast of mealie cobs - he
Pulled her on top of him and rolled her over
And fucked her as she grumbled about children
And daylight. Well, she'd reason. He paid
Extra. He enjoyed it more anyway, buying
These days.
     Walking home under coconuts
In the amber slatted light, he cursed
Marrying her cotton chastity, remembering
The breasts of the mother of his sons.
They were all he had now. They weren't bad
Kids, the little devils, and their mother's
Breasts and her brown compliance — why
Had he left them to marry this Portuguese?
Why *por deus* had he spent his savings on
A wife from Vila Nova with her cold silence?
His boys were all he had now. He would
Teach them volleyball, give them *his name*!
He walked on in wonder, his bootprints
Crushing on the sand the marks of hundreds
Of bare feet. Nothing had ever satisfied
Like this revenge. A landrover honked
Behind and he hitched a lift from a grinning
Black corporal. "You kill any terrorists?"
"*Sim*, bwana. Three by the bridge this shining
Morning. *Viva unidade*! *Viva the Republic*!"

5

Down river buried in a plumed
     island they drifted
     spinning

Three dugouts lashed together
     in a green noon
     humming with finches

29

down river, their bomb and the white baby turning slowly
    bends where herons
    angle-poise under fever trees

blanched with stork shit. Kingfishers
    slap water. A hippo yawns
    pink among peninsulas of lilies.

S.W. Hydra moulders in the shallows:
    history is last year's rust, this year's
    collapsing growth, but these

spinners of futures
    pass
    camouflaged in a floating island.

She sings to the baby:
    the men flick water
    on the green cloth over the hot bomb.

6

Crab-dancing, houseboy called it,
Paired-off sideways shuffle of white
Colonists preening. There was green
Wine and the oily clouds of sardines
On charcoal, of baby pigeons and peppered
Prawns. The *assimilado* band
From the sugar company upstream stunned
Clube Sporting with their amplified tremuloes.

Stroking his moustache the Governor
Sweated benevolence. The dancing was
Official. Officially the delta port
Where no building strained memory
Was 475 years old. Outside the residence
Camões sat in stone, his one eye
Mocking the hulks in the estuary. His plinth
Praised Da Gama who stole Odysseus' fame.

The People that this Country did possess,
Though they were likewise Ethiopians all,
Did more of Humane in their meens express
Then Those, into whose Hands we late did fall.
Upon the sandy beach with cheerfulness
They meet us, and with Dances Festival,
With them, their wives: and their mild Flocks of sheep,
Which fat and faire, and frisking they did keep.

From the pale jasmine by the steps
Houseboy watched. Madam, white-faced
Was being courted kindly: fox trot
With the Governor, glass of wine
With his lady wife. The room
Swam with heat and the sobbing
Blast of stacked chords. She choked.
Kindness was at her elbow. "*Por favor,*"

She said, "A moment only," spinning
To the verandah. The jasmine, "Madam,"
Querulous as a mosquito, "Madam,"
Showing his bald head. She gripped
The pillar, "Madam. Moises Ernesto!
Go to the church. Yourself. Now!"
He vanished, leaving her reeling
In the heavy fumes of sweet night jasmine.

7

Clanking as they pumped its handles the *jigga-jigga*
Shifted. Iron wheels groaned under the bomb's
Dead weight until momentum in the night air
Chilled sweat on their torsos. On the dark
Sand under the coconuts the narrow rails shone.
Rising and bowing in frantic ceremonial they
Hurtled through Mathilde nursing the fat tube
Of their revolution:

O —yo, baba, want-to-go
   pusha-pusha
O —yo, baba, want-to-go
   pusha garetta
O —yo, baba, want-to-go

                    It was perfect, hyena
Houseboy's plan perfect, breaching the port
By the main street like lazy bugger natives
Finishing tasks after the whistle. No tickets
For these bastards. *Jigga-jigga* helps home
Late niggers, lazy niggers, fuck-fuck, no
Tokens for the company store:

O — yo, baba, want-to-go
   pusha sairembo
O — yo, baba, want-to-go
                    The cold bomb
Unstoppable past the cemetry, the golf course
Airstrip, shooting the bailey-bridge over the inlet,
Sentries contemptuous, tossing their fag ends
Into the swamp, and dead straight under the lamps
The dual-carriageway to the target. In the *Clube
Sporting*, the band was Buddy Holly where
Isobel, white-faced, was leaving for the church.

8

Someone would like to have you
But I have you
      On a reed mat
      In a grass house
      In my mother's village.

Someone would like to bath you
But I bath you
      In the pool
      Under the *mpawa* tree
      In my mother's village.

32

Someone would like to feed you
But I feed you
    From a clay pot
    With my index finger
    In my mother's village.

Someone would like to carry you
But I carry you
    In a Zambia cloth
    On my back
    In my mother's village.

Someone would like to hold you
But I hold you
    On a grass mat
    In a round house
    In my mother's village.

9

He hadn't believed the friendly bomb
Would explode. When he saw the glow
In the customs house from the burning
Documents heaped round it, he smiled
At the comrades' simplicity. Then men
Ran yelling from the *Clube* and bullets
Whined. He watched Comrade China limp
Into the flames biting a grenade and the

Blast crashed him against the plates
Of the jetty. Rust coughed on his
Bald head and when he patted his lips
With the white handkerchief there
Was blood. Hyena houseboy. This man
A big stooge, isn't it! He studied
Blood and the white moon and knew
Anger beating in his temples like drums

And stood barefoot on the warm sand
Between the town of fires where tonight
It was wreckless to be black and the black
Estuary's beacon of moonlight. Fastidiously
He waded the shallows round the scuttled
Freighter and swam to the mangrove. His soft
Feet winced in the ooze but he swung like macaque
Through the coils of the crocodile inlet,

Crouching under the bailey bridge while
Landrovers drummed vengeance. Then the moon
Blinked and he panted to the churchyard.
The searchlight moon illumined her, the gun
Piercing her shadow. "They are all dead,"
"They've been summoned by their fathers."
She clutched her breasts with grief.
"Moises Ernesto?" "I saw her carry him".

The old man listened to the roaring
From the town, conscious of slender
Wrists and her stained tunic.
The whites had no religion. Blood
And the baby would not quiet
Their ancestors. His breath was
On her cheek. But torches clamoured
From the roadway and a voice houseboy

Feared. Bwana Ernesto, cheated
Of righteousness! Torches
Raged through the church gate
And she straddled to shoot,
Her buttocks steadied
By his thigh. "It's senhor," he hissed,
"Moises Ernesto's papa." But knowing
In his groin her melting hesitation,

He hugged the AK 47 and fired.

10

The first war was like this.
Sixteen years on it festers
Without character or courtesy.
Moonrise over the delta port shows
Coconut palms fingering old sores.
Beyond is a darkness of rumour. Fresh
Villagers join us, their horrors
Individual, the pattern cancerous.
Perhaps it will stop, perhaps get worse.
Meanwhile, the struggle is tonight's
Food. Bitter the war of brutalities
With incompetence, whose heroes
Are witches and blackmarketeers.

Headless outside the residence,
Poet of past glories, Camões:
Poet of fallen comrades, Camões.

THERE
(York)

Alice's Nasturtiums

At the walled garden's end in the gloom
of November's end they burn,
blood-orange trumpets
at the descent into winter.

The time-tearing wind has stripped
all but their passion.
They are luminous
in their layers of distance.

Do they couple in underground fires?
Have our ends stored summers
like a battery
fuelling these torches?

Their pale-leaf panda faces turn
to the light remaining.
At the first frost
They crumple like handkerchiefs.

The View from the Stockade

1

From the stockade is a view of pastoral
Lost, our fields and gardens
Wasted by the enemy.

For years the city appalled us but
When the hordes came where
Else was refuge?

From the stockade we watch thistles
Swarm. We have our wives here
And water. We shall survive

All but the heartsickness, our innocence
Undone. Now there begin
Ledgerbooks, usury.

2

"He's ca-ca-cantankerous," she stuttered.
It was her one English word
Almost, and where in Yorkshire did she
Find it, this Black woman
With her pig farmer, up
In the Dales? As she
Woke at five, mucked out the sties,
She swore back in Acholi
With a ripeness his mind shut out.

"He's ca-ca-cantankerous," she stuttered
To the Race Relations men
In her distress. There was nothing
They could do but open a file.
Why had she followed him
Home from the army? She had

Nothing to go back to. What silks
Did she expect? And he? What
Had he hoped to harvest of his rutting?

3

An old man striding, brittle in an anorak,
as weathered as his walking stick, his wife
in a duffle coat, hand on his arm, together
halt in Sampson Square, once Thursday Market.
"Once Thursday Market," he exclaims. "Aha!",
she says, brightening.

An old couple
discovering what they were looking for,
rhythms of pastoral in the traffic jams.

Lucy Poem

It always seemed there would be further
Springs, the river in flood, moorhen
And primrose, curlew and wild daffodils,
After the revolution back to the celandine.

Those teaching this were my present age
Then, ungratified, culpably eccentric:
After blood and drudgery there was mayflower,
This word being not nature but a text.

It isn't pylons crossing the wheatfield
That puts the pastoral out of fashion:
Whose heart can stop at a lagoon of bluebells
Without disclosing draglines of repression?

Always it seemed there would be fresh
Innocence, the river in flood, otters
And coltsfoot, pigeons and wild honeysuckle,
After the revolution back to Dorothy.

Joanna

1

The hardest part, writing the account
A dozen years after in another country,
The hardest memory was her utter
Separateness. She had lain in his arms
So soft, so pliable, he was the bridge
Straining above her, drowning
In her depths as she ebbed to the sea.
He was the leaky dam at L'Esperance.

Writing the account, her death made
Believable his lost age of gold.
But he knew it was never so. For
All the rich tapestry of poems
He wove round her, a fuck
Was a fuck. It left her untouched.

 2

I was slave, not so? The hardest
Part was he touched me with hope.
Not in bed as he pounded me
With his soft pestle, but after
When sweettalk could get him no more
And he sang his poems. He built me
A pool at L'Esperance by the gold
Waterfall. I loved him, nearly.

But he's just a man. No money, like
My father. Soon he'd want younger
Girls to pound out his pride, and where
Would I hide in England? So I laughed.
When he married I smashed my mortar
And drank my poison. And felt sure.

(*Joanna: the wife of Captain John Gabriel Stedman of Surinam*)

On the Train, Reading Dante

Halfway along the line we have to travel
I found myself in a siding outside Doncaster:
The sky was darkening, the land was level.

Both sides were fields of industrial waste,
Black water, derelict caravans.
To halt there and know the place exhausted

Brought on the old despondence.
Nothing so fine as wolf, lion or leopard
(That's money, pride or concupiscence

Piquant temptations!) stood
In the track. Nor was I in control
The diesel waiting at red.

As when the slaver's musket barrel
Flashed in the torchlight and the cave
Grinned with its cache of skulls,

The faces of corruption came alive.
Nearest the mouth, Appetite
With a toadstool as hors-d'oeuvre,

Wheeling its basket from the hypermarket
While the swollen-bellied, knob-
Jointed world's children cry out.

Second skull, Theory, a spider's web
Spun taut across the eye-holes:
Mechanical and merciless its drab

Dialectic. Next resident, Malice,
Smirking from a ledge (what minister fixed
Him there?) at blades and fibulas

Scattered on the cave floor, a chalk wrist
Reaching out, encircled by its amulets,
Supplicating Treachery, Violence

And Fraud. I remember the clay pots
Of millet beer, left in the entrance hole
To propitiate such malignant ghosts

As Dante Alighieri wrote to kill.
How thoroughly, without melodrama,
He marked down the lineaments of hell.

How solidly they live doing harm
To people who are known to me and I love.
Staring at my darkness I was calmer.

Then somewhere something happened, and I was moved.

The Precipice

Even from the precipice
we brought back
mementoes — a framed cartoon,
earthenware, a bloodstain of poppies.

Even in the furnace
we were hammering
moulds. Let me lie in you
shaped to your desiring.

Room for Autumn

We knew from the start this was a room
to listen to Brahms in. Westering,
watching the stockade wall at sundown,
it was a room for autumn and we tiled
one wall in yellows and cello brown
with poachers in the reed thickets
where the piano leaps peremptorily
bringing the falling fourths to resolution;
a room for books and a log fire
and love-making on the gold chesterfield.

Politics in the basement where the Irish
navvy lived blows its dust of a century
upwards. Through stretched chords,
long-fingered tenths, a dry harmattan
whistles. Bunched chromatic runs
from the gas lamp rising cannot
wall it out. We are restless having
witnessed blood. There is a fountain
daily over the narrow water where
murder is a hymn in sixteen bars.

Crafted music: the stockade at night
is the colour of the owl that keeps us
watching. We knew from the start
there would be trouble composing
a room hollowed out by all we have
lived through. Counter-point is one
of our words, tiles with their poetry
and the milk-white wall. And Brahms,
classicist with a dying fall. Autumn comes
even to the most unreconciled of believers.

On a Painting by William Etty

Towards the end he painted
Pheasants, plumed irridescent
Cock and drab hen together
Limp with apples and mirrored nuts
On an oak table.
                              This was
Long after London, his vast
Canvasses of allegory, when
Truth and Chastity came to Fall
With breasts so veined, so rosebud-tipped
ImpropriEtty, they joked.
                              The journeyman
Homed to Yorkshire where the gentry
Gunned pheasants. There is all
Sadness in this shattered
Wing, fushias, purples, yellow
Accusing iris.
                              Towards
The end he painted minatures,
Girls' faces mapped
With autumn, and these
Stiffening overdressed gamebirds,
Fruits, fruits.

For Her Wedding She Wore Her Breasts Bare

For her wedding she wore her breasts
Bare with woven beadwork at her waist
And plaited beadwork in her hair.
The girls sang, begging her
Never to leave them for the bridegroom's mat.
Her heart soared as they drew her to his hut.

In Leeds she wears a dufflecoat and headscarf.
Her straightened hair is shielded from the rain.
Her husband at the Poly studies husbandry.
He is proud his village wife wears dungarees.
She pushes her packed trolley round Tesco's,
Black, pregnant, angry, missing

Cowdung smouldering in the soft dusk as
Cattle praises echo from the kralls.
The woodsmoke curls from cooking fires.
The children demand stories
Or a lick of the ladle. Darkness drops.
The men come home in blankets with their pipes.

Per Se

With my cheque from *Poetry Wales*
she bought a bikini. Was Art ever
more rewarded, keeping
a steady eye on Nature?

The Archive

(after Jack Mapanje and for Adrian Hastings)

Loading the boxes in the hatchback, I wave
Adrian goodbye. It is a short drive
past Clifford's ruined Tower* to the archive.

Documents, an acquisition. This was
an important massacre. Our stock rises
with every scoop. The shelves bend in applause.

Not that Dinyero benefits, whose only
son the soldiers hacked down with Dinyero
watching. Or Elestina. Or Faranando cindered

in his hut as he struggled to save
Alefa his senile wife,
their bones shovelled in one hasty grave.

Nor could Falencha read the headlines
when her baby's precious brain
bespattered her grinding stone. The testimony

states such things. It was
an important massacre. It changed history
for the literate. We found in it new metaphors

for our own confusion, language borrowing
resonance from the harrowing
of the innocent as discord aped their sorrow.

The hatchback halts. We have moved
to other dramas. Only the archive
gathers the last gleanings of this harvest.

The ghosts of the villagers
whose fields are cratered by another war,
are dead as the dead Jews of Clifford's Tower.

(*Clifford's Tower: setting of the York Pogrom of March 1190*)

Suleiman the Merchant

Night snow, what light it burns,
Brighter than the wall, casting blue neon
Up at a low sky radiant with lamps.
These colours are magic, we have changed
Planets, pale grass, zebra trees,
Shimmering orange clouds like a child's
Or trader's vision or my own of purpose:

("Africa is a vast country," wrote Suleiman
The Merchant. "All the plants are black.")

A Prayer for my Son

It is a warm Sunday afternoon in January.
The Foss is ice-bound but the Ouse
Drifts, its pale islands unwinding.

Under the bridge the current, as snows
Shrink in the fells, accelerates. Slowly
Ice revolves in the pewter eddies.

I am driven. I walk within the walls
Streets burning with happiness
That Martin is well again on the hills.

Who could have known purchase
Would be like this? Up on the stray,
William, Henry and Ginger, he rallies

His gang, shins up a sycamore,
Argues, wins sententiously, chucks
Stones at an oil drum frozen in the reservoir

And loosens it. He unlocks
My own childhood from its boredom
Of Lord's day chapel and answering back

When khaki was God's uniform
And sin was being myself. Today
In the sun's release I claim

Jointly every courtyard and snickleway,
Skipping as he would the flagstone's
Hopscotch, praying that he too be

Given second chances. He is again
Well, and warmth is backing up
The Foss from the Ouse's surging:

— Chances to the seventieth hope
Time seven, but for which
I could not have found this partnership.

The Raft

Tossing in fever, heat breaking
from his forehead, he saw again
oval and delicate
framed in a sweat drop

her twenty-year-old face.
Beyond the heaving raft's
deck, repeated
as in a housefly's

eyeball, her face watched
from the flames. If he
stared she'd
sizzle. He must not focus.

Those years I held her beauty
like an egg. Today
I've sailed on
into her calm harbour.

The Highjack: an Epithalamium

1

The Boeing 707 highjack was for her
Memory. He explained that precisely
Through the intercom at Addis Ababa
With all the passengers still aboard.
This was for her, his dead wife
Though the flight deck swam and terror
Blanched his knuckles tightening on the grenade.

Refuelled, they flew on to Athens
Where he released to her wine
And sunlight all but the flight crew
And the President. This was for
Five years of her death in detention.
They simmered in the level glare,
The white terminal camouflaged by noon.

Terrorism, said the President coolly,
Was a manageable crime. He owned
The banks and the plantations. They
Had resources, it would take time.
The captain suffered, needing
Action, not this messy politics.
At nightfall, the intercom sang with demands.

Justice! The negotiators groaned.
A lunatic! But the gunman had plans,
The international court, councillors,
A mixed jury, the charge murder,
The President in the dock and three
Governments pledging their honour.
Checking, they found him on their computers,

Arrested in the Mall, frightening
Horses during the state visit
With a starting pistol. A file

At the F.O., the naturalised wife
Unprotected by her passport. Protest,
Minutes, marginalia, the agreed text.
Crassly, the dead offer of compensation.

A Greek functionary had the idea:
The co-pilot was married and a steward
And one of the hostesses with sons.
That second night the thought climbed
Hierachies, and the man sympathised,
Freeing the crew. So by morning, alone
With his enemy, he had saddened into error.

2

Full moon, guard her as she flies:
the air hungers
at such height: the cylinder
holding her is fragile:
no one knows what winds lurk
to whirl her into what spirals.

Full moon, as she flies, protect
from summoning desert,
swamp and jungle: ice
furs and clamps movement:
who can tell what armies wait
exacting what revenge for insult?

Full moon, shield her as she flies,
shine with superior
innocence on accident
and fevered malice: soot
seduces from the roof tops:
Goddess, light her swiftly home.

3

Alone with his warder, the President
Knew fear. In that hot tube,
Foetid toilets, stench
Thickening like smoke, it leaked
From his woollen banker's
Suit, tie, silk shirt, underwear hand-
Made his trunk the source of corruption:
Anything he unbuttoned the smell was worse.

He knew why. He was powerless.
He envied his tormentor in slacks
And casuals such purity
Of control. He had known it in jail
In the struggle when the sweet
Odour seeping from the latrine bucket
Was the air he lived on. He had smelt
It in countless others cowering at his feet.

Was the gunman's woman among
Them? How could he know? Thirty
Years he had studied
Power, and seized it, and then
Discovered how - that most things
Happened beyond his knowledge. His orders
Fluttered into swamps of incompetence
And rearing suddenly in ambush came events.

I want, he muttered, the latrine.
He heard his hoarseness and stumbled
To the first class toilet
Squatting with the door wedged open.
Latrine! this was power, to make him
Talk like a poor man without thinking.
What had justice to do with this crouching
To ingratiate himself? Couldn't the whiteman

Measure his absolute triumph?
Three days were enough to prove
Him expendable. Others
Would be trying out voices, there were
Others the banks could appoint.
What remained was flesh, his guts
Cramped with terror of the penalties
Of pain the whiteman's power would exact.

4

She gave colour to cities: London
was slate or mousy, Lisbon
ten varieties of clay and Athens
white, her face drawn always
upwards to the Parthenon.

She judged by restaurants: London
indoors, cloyed privacy, Lisbon
ten varieties of prawns and Athens
where part of the fun was
visiting the kitchens.

Below the Acropolis she discovered
their taverna. How could
he live without her eye for design?
How let her death linger,
something capricious?

5

In the soft dusk shadows quickened.
He ran to the flight deck, shouting
Down the intercom to pull
Back their troops. They
Swore faith but when he screamed
Again they complied. He knew
They were waiting, out in the half light.

There was one enemy and two
Threatened: himself and his prisoner.

This wasn't the drug. He had made
A citizen's arrest, responsibly,
Though his eyes ached
And he kept striding,
Striding. Voices he ignored.
There wasn't a politician in the world
He would cross the street for, nor
Policeman nor the psychiatrist
Whose honey drooled from the intercom —

Travelling they forgot colour.
Months went by innocently until
Professionals made it
A symbol, heightening
His tenderness. Then they were
Piano's black-and-white notes played
By? Soot seduced, the Parthenon glowed,
Oh Maria, yes, how she drew him
Into her joyfully and gave absolution.

Tinker, tailor, beggarman, slave:
There was a frightened black man
To protect, poor
Man. It was an error
Letting the crew go free. No
Politician cared about a black man
Grey with fear. Gladly he lifted
And with love the weight of history
For his black wife and her murderer.

6

Beyond them all
was the forest
humming with spirits:
in a sunlit clearing

61

houses with reed
walls and plaited roofs,
and the farms
spreading like green lakes.

Beyond them all
was the river
with green islands
turning in the current:
on the river
paths at dusk
women slender
with waterpots.

Cockcrow and children
and the husbands
planting, and wives
again to the river
as smoke unwound
from cooking fires.
In the forest
humming with spirits

crouched the hunter
with his charms:
duiker smooth
as an old hoe,
chimpanzee the drummer,
and buffalo before whom
unrequited the hunter
prostrates himself.

When they came
upriver by steamer
home, he was
ambushed by memory.
Within us all
is the forest,
the sunlit clearing
with houses and woodsmoke,

self-sufficient,
the generations talking,
the circle unbroken
by travel or trade.
Innocence dies
hard in the lover
when forests advance
on the spiked palisade.

7

So at midnight when the attack came
He was ready. He was standing
In shadow beside the open
Hatch above the gleaming pond of the wing.
Moonlight through the cabin window
Showed the President sleeping, shirtless.
Under the control tower vehicles
Huddled. The attack. he knew,
Would come from behind. The signal
Voices from the flight deck to distract him.

No, he was not Hamlet the terrorist
Nor Orestes. He had reached ends
And before him was
A wing like a column of moonlight on water.
I am Daedalus, he thought, I have
Challenged heights. The voices came,
Honeyed, mocking. He was startled,
Alert. He heard two soft thuds
And feet running. The explosions merged
Deafening as stun grenades blasted doors open.

Deliberately he stood in the moonlit
Hatch and the first shot spun him,
Falling in the silver
Pool, rolling, sliding, dropping again,
Embraced by the plane's black
Shadow on the tarmac. Sirens

Wailed, searchlights criss-crossed
Above him and he heard his balked
Attackers howling in confusion.
We have eluded them, he thought, and died.

That was the only ending. The President
Rules for life. The women praise him
For conquering, his
Portrait on their breasts. The bank's
Crisp black and white notes print
His picture too, on the re-issue
After the devaluation, the new loan
Paying interest on the old. Athens has
Other highjacks. The marksman relishes
His Order of the Mosquito, second class.

ALCABIDECHE
etc

A Mile or Two

A mile or two above the singing windmill
the full moon is sprinting
through marbled clouds.

The galloping moon
is in an ecstasy of pink marble.
The windmill sighs.

On Looking into Atkinson's History of Spain & Portugal

Here, Africa begins at the Pyrenees:
The population is Hamitic but

The Atlantic coast was settled before
Romans hammered Iberia foursquare

By wave upon wave of melancholy Celts:
One face looks to the Troubadors, one to Morocco,

One east to Virgil, one to the Brazils.
Who can resist such metaphors celebrating

Argument and green-wine coloured
Sunsets on the white facades of buildings

In the public squares where dark-haired
Men and girls walk hand in hand?

Why does this author fear them, heralding
Armies, budgets and the iron dictators?

Alcabideche

I put down my pen for a lunch of goat's cheese,
Bread, last year's wine and a melon, looking out
Across red-tiled terraces to fishing boats
Back this morning hours before I bought bread watching
The groomed and ironed girls trooping lovely to the city
And came home to writing. Then a siesta,
A walk and writing. I am doing
What I should like to do for ever. No,

There will be no second stanza questioning
This. These and children and you blossoming
Like morning glory on walls everywhere
Are all a man could need, and paper. As for
The makers of bread and red wine, I would
Trust them for life beyond the purveyors
Of varnished cork tiles or fish tanks or plastic
Flowers in the hypermarket on the Maginale.

Al-Qabdaq

(The pull of the soil was always very strong for the Andalusian poets who, for the most part, were of country origin ... Such was the case of Ibne Mucana al-Isbuni. Having lived at Seville at the court of the Abbadides, then at Grenada at the court of Zirides, he knew the inanities of the courtier's life and giving up the bogus fame of the royal salons he regained his village of Alcabideche, close by Sintra, to end his life cultivating his field. "I saw him", said one of his fellow countrymen who recounted to Ibne Bassam his encounter with the old poet, now deaf, his sickle in his hand. "I approached him and when I had taken him by the hand he made me sit down to look at the field in which someone was working before us. I asked him to recite some poetry and he improvised about the field.)

Dwellers at al-Qabdaq, husband well your seeds
      whether of onions or pumpkins.
A man of purpose needs a windmill turning
      with the clouds, not requiring water.
Al-Qabdaq doesn't produce, even in a good year,
      more than twenty sacks of corn.
Any more than that, the wild pigs come down
      from the forest in regular armies.
She is meagre with anything good or useful,
      just like me, as you know I have a poor ear.
I abandoned the kings in their finery, I refused
      to attend their processions and parted from them.
Here you find me at al-Qabdaq, harvesting thorns
      with my sharp and agile sickle.
If someone said, "Is it worth this trouble?",
      you'd answer, "The noble man's ensign is freedom".
Abu Bakr al-Muzaffar's love and good deeds were my guide
      so that I left for a garden in springtime.

(from the French of Henri Peres: Abu Zeide Mohamede Ibne Mucana, eleventh century Andalusian poet; Aby Bakr al-Muzaffar, Prince of Badajoz, d. 1068)

Surfaces

(for Jill & Alberto Dias)

I like the cool tenor of tiles:

the coolest place in *Largo de Camões*
is the tile shop. More even than the *livrarias*,
dusty and cavernous with riches, it holds us.

There is the sea in tiles:

dolphins, wine-carriers, marketeers, lilies,
discoverers and farmers,
are transfixed and transfigured

in a poetry of blue squares.

While the jangling trams snarl and gross fish
leer from the restaurant windows,
the houses are quiescent.

Tiles have burned their passions out:

they bring us back to surfaces, to dark wine,
a green bottle on a table cool with glaze,
afternoons of light and patterns:

tiles can be wiped clean endlessly.

The Difficult Art

"The most difficult art in the world," said
the *administrador* between mouthfuls, squid-prodding

fork raised, his right hand casting for the English words
(I thought of *ottava rima* and Camões),

"is the art of choosing a good melon."
Camões sits in his praza under the pigeons.

His poetry is fired hard like tiles:
his round eye ridicules the end of empire.

To be fair to my friend (retired) the grilled squid
Was succulent in the club where they planned the coup.

Everything that summer was like the wild melons
exploding at a touch to scatter seeds.

Pan

Late afternoon with his five
Tinkling sheep he staggers down
The slope to the cabbage patch
Behind the hedge of ripe blackberries

And squatting behind the garage
He sings. We know he is singing
Because his mouth moves and his
Hands wave in rhythm and his legs jerk.

Five sheep and a song. From our
Tiled verandah we watch his ecstasy.
Shadows of the gnarled cabbages
Lengthen to his feet like palings.

Farewell green fields, farewell
Ye happy groves! He gestures
With his bishop's crook, roping
His five sheep, leading them like dogs.

Travelogue

The Selective Traveller in Portugal
By Ann Bridge and Susan Loundes
Is busily, informedly, hopelessly
English — in short, a classic. Even
The title's modest disclaimer (to select
Is to be select) bemuses, like tweeds
And advance enquiries and sensible shoes.
What lovely years they had!
The ladies are just a little loud,

But what a world they lived in.
Dead kings, priests, artists and peasants
Harmonised perfectly under the dictator.
As they left the old palace or the misericordia
After inspecting the exceptionally fine ceiling
Or roundly condemning the brown tiles,
There were lace-makers on the pathway
Or farmers with grape-stained legs
And pretty girls and a soldier.

It is Bloomsbury out of Baedeker,
It is the start of an old opera (though
If that trio gets up to its tricks
Nanny will put a stop at once
To such nonsense!) It should
Also be mentioned that the ladies
Are uncomfortable with poets. None is
Selected unless safely entombed
In tiles or paint or in memorial sculpture.

The Box

I parked outside the hospital in Luis de Camões
And waited. I was coaxing alive a poem.

Two men with a coffin went inside:
Fifteen minutes later I had changed a tense.

Four men, two in tee-shirts, one with a cigarette,
Shouldered the coffin into the hearse. The two stood back,

Dusting nothing from their hands, easing their shoulders,
Refusing thanks "for nothing", and crossed

The road to the cafe, ordering *aguadente*.
The poem clicked suddenly like a shut box.

✕Do Tempo Perdido

(after Sebastião da Gama)

Before we left I watched for two hours
Darkness closing on our golden beach.
It began with the cliff's shadow

Sliding along the bright sickle, touching
The bathers and the lovers who rose
Separately and dressed. It stretched

Out across the emerald waters so
Clear you could stare
Down fifty metres and see

The fishing boats silhouetted
On pale sand. You could see mackerel
Hovering and the drifting tresses

Of water plants. Then darkness clicked
And the sea became only the mirror
Of an olive sky and of lights flickering.

I watched for an hour the colours
Of that surface. Perfection
And effort and error

Are a loss beyond irony.
I could see houses and the fishing boats,
Whitewashed and pantiled, or painted

Every colour, giving out lights
All present in the poem
Of the sea's surface, and defeated.

Olive became pewter, hardening
To blacklead, and still
The oil murmured.

I asked for the bill
And you wrote a cheque
And we struck the steep hill

Into the night without speaking.
From the summit
The sea was a void, beckoning.

Lamps in old vinyards
Blessed our hurtling
Down converging valleys to our bed.

Antonio Rui

Antonio Rui whose township mother was always,
grinned the white managers, available
                              if you were desperate,

Rui, born in the *bairro*, father unknown,
with a cleft palate, a game leg, and sores
                              corrupting his eardrums,

would hobble the track between tin-roofed shanties
where women sweated at mortars or dragged behind them
                              huge water barrels,

with a watch strapped to his left wrist, a transistor
clapped to his right ear, gold teeth smiling, his shades
                              reflecting coconut palms,

and jabbering, stammering in tortured Portuguese
of a Grundig next year, a Suzuki, an outboard motor,
                              a Boeing 747 to Lisbon,

and we shared the joke. What worked and gleamed
he worshipped. People being flawed irreparably,
                              gadgets were his ikons.

Today, years on, earphones, Grundig, digital watch,
we mèt him hobbling in *Largo de Camões*, as voluble
                              with images as ever:

next year he will cross the Tagus, next year
a beach house for his mother, next year the white men
                              will make him *chefe*.

For Abu Zeide Mohamede Ibne Mucana

Not fifty yards from my verandah
is a windmill, and another
behind the *oliveira*, and a third

by the marble quarry. They face
outwards, humming separately
in the companionable winds of dusk.

Where else in Alcabideche
should I hunt for you, Mucana,
in the village named in the language

of your poem? In pantiles
or *azulejos* or blue-dyed stonework?
In the geography of pure white walls?

Not in the cool church, but surely
in the waters beneath it
springing even in August.

I have heard of your poem
in praise of our village christened
in the language of your poem.

Another tongue celebrates
still Christ's blessing
on your defeat,

and your poem
is silenced,
having no home.

But there is a memory of your windmills,
of water swelling marvellously
in onions and melons,

79

in pumpkins so special
even Christ
would have smacked his lips.

Yesterday, we ate Domingos' pumpkin
from the summer garden
below the spring,

And Mucana, your windmills spun
from your own soil
in another alien language this other poem.

The Awning

Late summer brought Atlantic gales:
The beaches whitened, charcoal fires

Flew wild. Behind our shutters we talked
Suddenly of winter. Research

Reveals, announced the team on TV,
There are 2229 basic Portuguese words.

Artur and his children came to dinner:
Jailed by one side, exiled by the other,

He has been angered into cold action.
Afterwards at the window I ate grapes

Spitting seeds into the swirling darkness.
Across the praza under the flapping awning

A man and woman lingered over wine.

Charcoal

There is a moment when the wood has caught
and the charcoal has done its tinkling
and glows lasciviously, when
the carafe of *Dão* or *Quinta da Bacalhoa*
simmers in our talk
of long delayed summers peering
down at long last down
our well between the terraced houses
north north north
on our tiles and towel of lawn,

there is a moment when the fumes of burning
lamb with oreganum, bay leaves and onion,
drift across the rag of lawn
to the brick wall where I'm reading
Walcott or Sebastião da Gama
or Dafydd ap Gwilym slagging
January, purring over May
and his burning trysts
in the improbable holly bush,
at that moment all our summers merge

in a scent so quick I don't know
what I'm remembering but, before
reductive words, happiness
floods, stinging my eyelids,
and I walk to where you are turning
skewers and I hold
your waist while you press
my wrists with your elbows:
all summers with wine and charcoal
are dark with south and south is you.

Immortal Diamond

(Jack Mapanje, detained 25 September, 1987)

Outside the bar, night, bullfrogs promising rain,
the sky a dome of stars ripped
by the black edge of the mountain.

Bloated face, trunk like a baobab,
"We've got your lame friend,"
from the unmarked jeep

boasting Special Branch. Words hidden
a hemisphere off grudge
"Now you're on your own,"

and I can smell here the Carlsberg
on his breath. He leers
from the smuggled page.

Lame: alone: "we're
preparing a place for him."
This clown knows the power

of pauses, the ecstasy of rhythm.
His threat is accurately
their dread. For Jack, our dear friend's poems

are out, unparoled, his meta-
phors dancing from lip
to lip and no heavyweight

knuckles ripping
pages
can stop

them. The crippled swagger
"We've got your friend,"
calms outrage

at that night, that frog-loud prison yard, leaned
on by the mountain, where Jack, joke, patch,
matchwood, hardens

like starlight, needing no crutch.